INIQUITY FERVOR

THE DUCHY OF DISPOSITION

SUMEET KUMAR

Sumeet Kumar

Sumeet Kumar , A adult who experiences many phases of life , a well known writer and a writer of new era. In reality he is a writter as well as singer (as a hobby) and a standup comedian . Very exciting and interesting fact about him is that he is author of New era i.e. he starts his journey of writing at the age when he was going to schools to get the study . His streak of 100 books will be the great achievement for him in future. His some famous works i.e. Maturity Of Love (Genre - Love),Privacy For Dream (Genre

- Middle Class), Army Squad ofLove (Genre- The Seperation of Army Love), 5 Days of Love(Genre- Temporarily Love), Th e Endearment Of Love(Genre - Historical Era Of Love), Social Destruction Indo-Pak (Genre - The Story of The Love At The Time Of Division Of India And Pakistan), Middle Class Soul (Genre - The Dreams of Middle Class), The Accursed Kanatpur (Genre -The Horrific Story Of A Village), Wrong Number (Genre -The Suspenseful Physco Killer Story), The Secrecy OfDeadly Midnight (Genre - The Suspense About a Crime),Fragile Religious Of Death (Genre- The Death Of A TrustfulPerson), Nature Vs Science (Genre - The Future Battle Between Nature And Science In A Horrific Way), Generic Man (Genre - The Dream of I.I.T), The Unconsious 12 Hours(Genre - The Illusion At Stage Of Comma), The StrangeBurden (Genre - The Burden Of Love) , Her Existence (Genre- The Female Pain In The Society) , Jockstrap Prize (Genre -The True Story Of A National Athlete) , H Man [Hindi] (Genre - Superhero Tragic Story), H Man [English] (Genre - Superhero Tragic Story) , Maturity Of Love [Englsih] (Genre - Love) and many more are available on various geners on the offcial platform of **Amazon, Flipkart and Notionpress**. You can buy them from there.

Contents

Acknowledgements

Aman Kumar

Special Thanks to **Aman Kumar** who worked so hard in the preparation of this book. He has continually put with my passive voice, omission of words, and late night calls. You have been wonderful. Thanks to him for his precious time in reviewing proposals , individual chapters and early drafts, along with his suggestions on the applicability of the material to the world.

I
StrangeFul People

I Know that there are some such paths in life which
have no destination, they try to lane their love in the
gathering just for the sake of show and its only one truth
whose love is very beautiful When you can't maintain a

relationship, why do you make it undefined In the eyes of the world, you all see that we are neither Romeo, Juliet, nor Heer Ranjha, we are also in love for each other, we also give our lives for each other. I can forgive my lover, if those who have these thoughts, they will never say the path, no love, the things that teach people to live, their devices do not work, yet they provide oxygen at the time and some things are not even today I understood that if there was love earlier, then hatred is the meaning of my love, without which you can never fulfill the nature of living, without it today you are famous in your happiness in the gathering why undefined what right do you have to ruin someone To find the reason for your happiness in your own gathering? It is strange that this people is also undefined and their love importance was very illegitimate, which nowadays does not stop in any one arm, when she left me, she only told me that she cannot maintain the relationship anymore, she broke in the bash. Because of the loss of any one witness, we forget our whole world, our happiness, our own love and our own smile undefined.

"Your love is so much painful , my love
That it is near me everytime but didn't have a
power to come across with me, my love "

.If God is the punishment for every crime in the world, then why is it not for love, why those person forget us so easily and leave their friends with us and say that you have to live and be in good health, those times their love is ours. Do not think about their sympathies, which we consider to be lovely and try to know closer to them, I had done the same way, the farm is still the whole story and the alphabet is a little work and the respect of the time is also good journey Seeing that, he tries to know about her. Till then I didn't feel anything special in my studies, my friends used to get calls many times, yet I did not wake them up at all because they were not round the clock, they had become lifelines for me, at that time whenever the morning rays came to my eyes. Remembering him at the foot party every time, doing baatio was like a profession. It is not a new thing that the love that I had given me, not everyone would have given it, if the witness is good, neither it is good for it, I have said it earlier also, Even after being busy all the time, I always used to get calls from him, not because I was in love with him, that is because he should leave me and go away because these accidents have happened to me many times because human wealth can never buy love. Even if you have two moments after looking at your wealth, it is not possible for a lifetime, if someone is addicted to body, then someone has to share and I also knew what he had to say. After two months, we used to meet each other many times and day and night, after three months, the distance and depth of the sages became true. I had a lot of longing for her pond, she gave me those things, love, care, which people also call care and time which is very important for making a relationship strong. He used to think about mirror words

and used to remember him in many times because of his friendship, he used to say that he was not like others Yes, she will always be with me and to be honest, she has become very passionate about her future, started thinking about her future. For I also lost the land which I used to feel safe in the shadow and it was in such a condition that I fought many battles to secure it. Fought and in the end when I fought with him, I was hurt, I am telling so many things, what is the truth after all? If after this option any such tradition comes to the fore, then let him know because he is never wrong, no witness can affect your happiness, not your compulsions and I came to know when I was separated from him, sorry I was separated It was. After about a month, that too after spending some time together, after sharing our past memories with each other, there is a rift between us. I started fighting, that means both of us did not know the reason for that, it was probably mine because I had become too secure in the beginning and atleast the end of my life , so he could not understand his condition, what is he saying after all, so it started when his calls Messages stopped coming, whose habit she got lost in some pall, so my nature had understood that she is no longer with me, neither she tried to understand nor I did not talk for one day before understanding then two days again At the time of the week, the silence was growing inside me, I did not understand what it was, never had the courage to express my feet, she said that you are also my family, I can leave my family, my feet are not you, I am every time Lamha Bash used to ask her all things that if your family didn't accept me then undefined then only I could see her tabusam when she said with great love that she should marry me in undefined. I am not even able to write these words well because when those accidents which happen in my laughter I was imprisoned somewhere, now he does not seem to be safe, man has given so much toad that in eight months my words are also giving me trouble, then it was separated. When he did not call me for many softs, then I finally messaged him and asked if there is anything undefined You are neither messaging me nor any call I have made any mistake is undefined If yes, please forgive me, I have no say to trouble you, that's why you're not getting the conversation, so feeling weird, feeling a strange perfect silence that I can't handle <what to do undefined I don't understand if there is any reason, tell me undefined at the moment he said enough to me . I didn't even say anything to him at that time. enough remained silent undefined because at the time I had understood that it is going to break, which means that the foundation of the relationship is going to be broken now she has told me to separate. I have made my own, he doesn't care about me, that bash is looking for the right time to leave me and is lucky that my ismat gave him that reason too undefined.

CONVERSATION

"

ME : *Why are you not doing talk with me , if there is a problem, then I will not tell you how to fix it, for so many days, we have not even talked, well leave that, you are fine, and what about your leg , is it fine, how are you, eating, even idiot undefined*

SHIKHA : ....

ME : *well what are you doing Buggu sorry na man sorry I was a little sick so I did not forgive you for many days please*"

.At that time there was silence and it was also known that now she has become very far away from my arms, she does not feel like my words are like before. It is already done, even after being close to me, I have become very difficult, I was too scared at the time that she should not say that she should not say that she should not say that she is not her own, she should not say that for which I am not ready. enough was asking so much at the above time that I wish it was not that day, Lord, let me break the teachings today because I am not ready for this, this banda will break even if she is called the sepration then even then my luck can change. The feet were saying to him that he was still there, he had left me on the very first day when I told him my compulsions when he became aware of my love because he was very rude, every time bash used to fight with everyone. Witness is a question, is it not the fault of those people, because of which they have lost everything, what is not the reason for undefined in which even today, as before I can't be created and if my condition is like this then who is behind it is not there Whatever I was, I told all that my compulsions, my love is the reason for my anger, everything is still there, yet he said so much to me that goodbye! lo manta now the story is about to end foot before her.

> **"SHIKHA** : *I m quit.*
> **ME** : *Quit what ? this relationship ?*
> **SHIKHA** : *Yeah this relationship*
> **ME** : *.......................*
> **SHIKHA** : *Ok bye .* **"**

What did everyone say to her that I can't live without you in my life, I can't go to death, tried to die, but fate didn't accept my grave, he told me to go by saying that now you have to bear more and many deceits. Whoever you want to see with your own eyes, also said while laughing that whatever you want, you can give as much trouble as you say, because my anger is meeting you for two moments, he has his own regret, so how can I return to it? , I say to erase every moment, before leaving, those who keep me attached to her, every memories and those moments too, I tell you to tell the unfinished story of the conversation that if she is reading my donation, then you will have your gathering. Congrats and we have lost my happiness in part too.

"I have found a gift in love
That somewhere she is getting married with
someone
And somewhere in graveyard a date
announces for my grave"

II

The Love in Dead

I am trying to write today, my condition is not good, that means I can't do alot of conversation because the words of time are not that much, age has no limit, if a person gets the right love to live, then he can live for many years. Can kill and can also kill, it is said that there are three types of person in the world, one who would live with the infidelity that they have found in love and on the other side the story of the possible way is innumerable and on the third side they would take China by faith. It is when the human race was born in the world of God, so it was not a matter of love that someone says that the land whose handwriting foot we wrote our destiny and our mother earth, a mother's love can never go away from you. Nor can she ever leave you, people don't know how many names they call a love, if one thing is common in all of them, then it is just waste What happens to us is undefined who is the right destination, which path and any kind of infidelity, if humanity loses in front of someone, then it is not only itself. Loses his own existence in front of the world Can't feel inside nor ever try to get it I sit by saying that no one can express my pain to anyone, nor can anyone feel it Maybe, if we see love by connecting it with science, then its love is completely different, it will never be able to meet with each other, nor will it ever be able to connect with each other because its theory is the only artificial which we have made, science has not created it, has anyone ever Have seen and heard that Albert Einstein was caught yesterday in a park with his beloved. I am not undefined nor undefined while giving my love, this love neither comes in your feet with the recommendation of pain, nor does it become your politics because we have made it, it is not a small thing at all, which I am saying why Whoever the age is more than that, by taking many kinds of deceit and what are these emotions undefined, there are many such things that we get because of just one love, do they have any meaning in the undefined world if someone If there is any cost, then only the mother who gave birth and the other male father who taught you to walk, she is not even in love with her feet. It is because their fight is above all.

*"**I am very much secured in your lap , mom**
Everything was ok , mom*

The thing that i missed everytime is your care ,
mom
You have a inborn talent of reading some
stuffs in my mind , mom ”

No one has any say in breaking because it is the custom of every witness that they should be happy and they should maintain their smile, which has been taken away from them because of some other witness, if the world is human, then there is no need for love. To live because the world of the child is already included in the form of humanity, so what is the need of second humility, well my words are giving trouble to me, I can neither express it nor express it anymore Can make my feet famous, my love can never be forgotten with the help of those friends, that's why today I am going to tell every secret whose love forced me to break my legs undefined I am revealing my whole story in half part, maybe some logs can't understand Because the relief of pain is not available to everyone in one part The logs in love leave their anger, so everyone says that they will die on the day of love. The first wind of the lamp blows, it is very difficult to say about burial sites or act of god , often those people whose love remains incomplete. It was missing, it was unknown, everyone knows about the ruin, yet the love of the heart, which is always there, would have been ready for me that what we consider to be our whole world, it is only a dream, the whole gathering of our dreams is a witness that one After leaving a modest person, the world becomes desolate,

There was no news that there would be such a pair of feet, to tell the truth, the day I met, I had thought that my dear brother had undefined feet after that, when he left, then life had changed, moments changed my habit, which I can't even forget.

Even today's gathering had changed with a heart. I didn't even know if he would come back to me again, in my blessings, that is the silence of the feet, the silence of the face now says not to leave the lonely soul, today I felt that in my heart My friends can never be true, I can't even call them a deceiver, because I had chosen them, I had adopted their love, I never understood the fortunes of luck, what do they say and what is their handwriting. Maybe now that many you have missed me, every time I am giving myself a consolation and the turn is my destination, feet, they come back again, I wish we could express our love with each other's eyes and feet. Is this possible? summon can be accepted undefined foot may not be possible because now that donation is incomplete

Now my hatred has become summon for me and a kind of burial sites also but now that anger is included by seeing which I used to tell myself all the time that I am worthy of you For the first time we were unaware of each other's feet when I met him, I used to tell him that he should be involved in my part all the time, my love became my habit.

Now I don't say to look, maybe he is right today by being wrong and I am wrong even after being right I may not be able to tell everyone, because I was not even used to it, I am not able to understand whether this love is some kind of love, which I say to forget, it is okay, now I will not remember him, I will never meet him I will do my self a thousand words and stay away from him, will I really be able to stay away from him, what is the truth of my pronounciation, who is just saying that you forget him, now his world is different by remembering him and how can I forget your world. Every time I ask why I have to give up the habit, he has my love for him too, so why can't I accept it? Nana I wish I could try to make her feel happy again, I can bring her in my part Now she gives reason for silence Even I am alive, why am I not feeling like this, today this is not the first time it has happened at all, because I have a habit of loneliness, why do I feel that way again? I can start a new life, handwriting is incomplete, parts are also incomplete, feet are really incomplete, so many questions are roaming around that I do not even have an answer, after all, what should I say to my anger undefined Who is right, I should do it in my own part. Not the man who used to get it because of a witness, now I am the sixth to get rid of my habit, it is not possible that I do not know, this whole world is not worthy of me, it is probably not worth it, I will not live without it Even with myself, if my luck does not include the grace of grace, then what is the use of forgetting to say to someone else, to every witness that has started the trouble, is it possible to forget the past that I myself I have made even the solitude of time, ruins a person, I say to do a lot, I say that my feet inside me, I tell myself to fight and I say to move forward, I have forgotten my feet, which is the right destination, cash, happiness, everything Maybe now I don't deserve it, I have taken it, maybe now I don't deserve anyone, even my anger knows what foot really is because because of one person neither my life changes nor your dreams then my Who was the correct handwriting in life that God had included, even after saying that he could not erase it

?

**"*By loving you , i am not able to love you*
*i am not able to understand you***

INIQUITY FERVOR

you are so much beautiful but i am not able to stare you"

III
Wheedle

I had heard earlier that people sacrifice themselves to get their love, today I have seen that truth with my own eyes and I also say to do the left, if the relationship is added in a hurry, neither can it be broken at any time because one cannot grow up. He is not in love, nor does he become a friend of anyone, even if he becomes a lover by mistake, it can only be made in China, everyone's fate is not written in his first love writing, if there is no second foot, then if he is a close relationship If you are not ready to fulfill, then can there be any such reality, I think it is a matter of love, if you fall in love with someone, then tell him your compulsions mat, which you have suffered for years, show that too mat because Your rudeness will get angry with you at that time, I had told everything about my past and future in my part. If someone doesn't do it, will someone choose? Witness is my pure family manta undefined has given her so much love that she has no partner If the roads are difficult, then logs often forget their destination, those who cannot forget their feet, they work hard to get them, this thing is a completely wrong thing called hard work, feet are not at all for love, otherwise today there are no person like Ambani.

In the world because his wealth has become his first love, well I do not say to repeat the accident again, it is okay if he is not with me, the arms whose wealth has been given to him, will he be able to give him that happiness this time Will someone else's arms keep him safe the way I used to keep him safe.

**"*I don't have much time to spend*
And you don't have enough sympathy to
spend"**

5 SEPTEMBER , When I met her for the first time, I saw her many times even before this, I had a different day's bailout, because the covid season was going on, so whenever she came, she would bring her protective husband with her, I mean to say Our masks We met for the first time in our

coaching center and how: you all know what you met undefined If you don't know then let me tell you that Teacher's Day party was going on this day so we both met for the first time because I was a senior and he was not my junior, why was my heart's affection changing all the time seeing him? Saw the time would have said, could have told him directly that I have become in love with you, how did it happen, I do not know why bash is love to you I was in public, yet why my words were not coming out in front of him, why was feeling nervous in front of that beautiful girl who was first I had made my heart beat a little too fast by looking at the bar, is it true that I often do a lot of madness in the people legs, which is probably right in the right part, I have also done many madness and today the same madness Paan many results in front of me whom I am not ready to believe at all Not taking the name of leaving and seeing her eyes on one side, which I still go crazy on seeing feet, I wish I would have rocked myself on this day, neither would have said this nor this love. Toh left, then the matter happened such a day that I saw him then he saw me then I saw the baton's feet. It is the world that is not as unemployed as many souls are beyond those who wash their feet after a girl in such a way as if she is a nymph, she is from heaven. I have come some innings, for the first time, I could understand in the bottles that love is also like a government job, whose sentence comes out so many feet, not everyone could qualify it because many logs get spread in its entrance exams itself At the time, we all were riding the same nine legs, which means preparing for the same government job, the result was going to be the same because at that time only one word was left in the post of lover, which was not known to whom? Not told, I am Atulya singh, who is from Bihar, even though I do not know the language of Bihar, it means that my father is a government employer from Maghai, my mother is a housewife and we also have a big family in which my role is played. It is that I am the shortest, my relationship, the length of my feet is nothing special, my feet are worth working for Because neither it has algebraic calculations nor it is any maths subject, well I did it Didn't even tell the name of girl, on seeing it for the first time, I got the silence that I am facing till today and maybe even further, so the name of his witness is nothing but Shika Singh which means both of us have the title Same but It does not mean that we are brothers and sisters, enough is used by all the students in my house; Let's see further that my story last day, who got a government job, means learned that love had some luck, so we were decorating our classrooms all day and I was sitting silently, I was nervous that how did he talk about his heart:

Because whenever my bastard friend asks him to say something, every lawyer gives me some work and insults me so much that today my mind has become too hard to get a girl. maybe find them and then friendship is like a conversation and also its songs like

" Where is a friend like you" Well now leave the word of friendship and Let's forget what happened in the end, what happened now?
I knew that now my lentils will not melt at all due to my friends, that's why I thought that I would be silent, that's why it was also true at the time that if I had I should save my friends too undefined What should I do, I loved my friendship so much I called sir and said sir we have decorated the class room now bash you will come and cut the cake, I didn't use shishtone feet It didn't even work for

some things, because they were waiting for a long time because a mistake was made, then after that the head entered, then the cake was cut, after that everyone had a full breakfast and after that again everyone did the speech. After that everyone was going home that I told him that you do Instagram to him, then he said, what crime did I do while doing all that then I said that I do not mean to say something to you I have to do, I can do it, so you do not, who did not think about you, I knew that she knows that I want something from her, feet and She was troubling me and knowing that I was acting upset with her conversation, after that I immediately gave her the book of James Bond and said that my Eid is there, tonight, there would be more lights. That's when the head asked him to leave saying that the night was enough, now go home, what can I say, the feet were getting so angry, he went quietly in his feet and could have done it even if he did something. Hanging me upside down I am joking, after a few days I had left my upper legs that if I get it, then it is fine and if I do not get it, then like life was going on, before its arrival, I will move my car forward That too on two wheels.

I never thought that my love would be accepted so soon in his gathering. If the feeder rhythm of being accepted would have been given, then I would not have been so devastated today in his memories because when I expressed love in front of him Why did he not even think about anything and enough has spoken, I knew that this love is not a thing May my luck be good, that's why my hard work has paid off, this day I understood two things and even today those two bags are doing me a favor. Even if you take care, he will feel sorry for going away from you, I mean to say that it is not a Jat and the one who plays it has no place. The very next day he messaged me and said can we meet Maybe I had said these things, she also said it is a happy time, when we met for the second time, that means, the next day, she was in a simple Indian dress, meaning to be a true believer, seeing her happy time was undefined and this thought I had taken my future wife's feet, they say that thinking is only the sweetheart of dreams, not of reality.

After all, I was more delusional when he held my hand in front of everyone, what does it mean to say that I was so nervous that I Hands were also not working for some time, then when he saw the whole society and society saw us, then he left his hands a little distance. I both went to the temple to become famous in the faith of God, after that both of us sat alone for a lot of things, then I told her about my past, she got a little angry after listening to her and at the happy time she said that when you stay with me I'll do a job Was saying that and was also saying that it is! The gardener has changed my fate only and now when I believe those things, he did not keep himself safe, his friends and my sister-in-law are still clearly visible by writing this. He is no longer with me, I am tired, I now say to go on such a journey where neither his friends nor he is jealous nor he is abusive

"The Love doesn't have a house , it always
residing sometimes someone's home
And sometime's other's home"

"How she is now in the love
Don't ask me in turn because i am just alive in
love"